Stress Management
A Holistic Approach

5 Steps plan to manage Stress in your Life

By

Subodh Gupta

Corporate Trainer

First Edition February 2008

Copyright @2008 by Subodh Gupta

All rights reserved. No part of this publication may be reproduced, stored or transmitted in any form or by any means without the prior written permission of the Author.

ISBN 978-0-9556882-1-8

Published by
Subodh Gupta
+44(0)7966275913
Head office: London (UK)
Email: info@subodhgupta.com
Website: www.subodhgupta.com

Publisher Note:

The reader should not regard the recommendations in this book as substitute advice of a qualified therapist. The aim of this book is to create awareness among the masses about Stress and a practical approach to come out of it.

Acknowledgements

I am grateful to my parents and all my teachers who taught me at various stages of my life & shared with me their wisdom.

Content

Introduction   6

Section 1: Understanding all about Stress

What is Stress?	11
Whether Stress is Good or Bad?	12
Effect of Excessive Stress in your Life	14
Most Common Reasons for Stress	16
Symptoms and Stages of Stress	20
Ineffective Way People Try to Cope with their Stressful Situation	21
Why People are not able to Solve their Stress Related Problems?	22

Section 2: Understanding & Training Mind

Life & Issues	31
No Problem is Permanent	37
No Complaining	39
Present Moment	41
Desires	42
Internally Driven	44
2 weeks Schedule Training Mind	46

Section 3: Five Practical Steps for Managing Stress

Step 1: Identify the Cause of your Stress   49
Step 2: Understand and Accept the Reality   55
Step 3: Collect all the Possible Information   58
Step 4: Focus your Attention on Solution   61
Step 5: Action   66

Stress Management a Holistic Approach   69

Yogic Wisdom about Managing Stress   74

Introduction:

Congratulation Friend,

The very fact that you are reading this book is a sign that you are a progressive person who just does not want to sit back and allow himself /herself to be controlled by circumstances; rather you are a kind of person who would try to take action to come out of it.

I am sure you would come out of your stressful situation sooner or later because of your attitude.

In the present day highly competitive environment changes are taking place at breathtaking speed. Life has become never ending race against time, technology apart from uncertainty.

This eventually results in anxiety and creates tension especially for those who are not able to cope with the changes. This fast life becomes more complicated if someone lacks skills in other area of life, for example personal relationship, social skills, etc.

All this leads to stress on mind and body level and the individual starts losing health as well which makes the situation more complicated.

However, I strongly believe that if there is a problem then there has to be a solution and this book is all about solution.

This book is based on practical life experiences and it is to the point. The purpose of this book is that once you have finished reading it you are ready to come out of your stressful situation no matter where you are in your life.

This book consists of 3 sections. The section 1 is all about Understanding of Stress from various perspectives, section 2 is about Understanding and Training the Mind and section 3 is about acting upon the five practical steps for Managing Stress.

I would recommend you to first read the sections 1 and 2 before moving on to the section 3 as it is easier to solve any issue if you understand it fully.

You may have any kind of problem or issue in your life, once you follow the 5 steps described in the section 3 of this book you are on your way to Stress free life.

May all being be free from Stress.

Subodh Gupta

8

Section 1

Understanding all about Stress

"When one door is shut, another opens."

-- Miguel De Cervantes

What is Stress?

Stress is the kind of feeling or disharmony which develops when you do not achieve what you want. Stress develops when the mind of a person overpowers his/her thinking capacity or when desires and attachment overpower capacity to discriminate.

It is an internal reaction and it depends upon how we interpret external situation and if it is negative, it results in building up negative emotions or energy inside us.

Same problem in life can have different level of Stress for two different people depending upon how they perceive and handle the situation. If an individual lacks the ability to deal with the situation and he is not able to relieve the Stress reaction, stress becomes distress and transforms itself into disorder at mind and body level.

Whether Stress is Good or Bad?

Stress can be both good as well as bad. While some Stress is normal and even necessary, in fact healthy for increasing your work related productivity, too much of it over period of time can affect your health.

Stress can either help you to improve your performance or it can hinder your effectiveness depending upon your stress level.

Like in musical instrument, if enough tension or tightness in not there, the instrument will give unpleasant music, however if there is too much tension or if it is too tight it may lead to breaking up of a string. Optimum amount of tension in the string will give the pleasant music.

In a similar way it works with the human being, if people do not have any deadline they become inefficient however at the same time very strict deadline and pressure effect their health and productivity severely. You can see people who are working in sales, project management, etc. are mostly stressed as they are chasing tight deadlines all the time in this fast competitive environment.

"You don't get ulcers from what you eat. You get them from what's eating you."

--Vicki Baum 1888-1960

Effect of Excessive Stress in your Life

Have you wondered what can be the damaging effect of stress in your life? You might be surprised to know that it can affect almost every area of your life. For example:

Effect of Excessive Stress on your Work can lead to:

Lowering productivity or performance

Affecting your team work as you could be more irritated because of Stress.

Effect of Stress on your Health:

Your personal health care cost may go up because of stress (*In fact Stress has already become the second biggest cause of employee sickness absence days in the UK*).

Stress if allowed to persist can be the major reason for irritation, backaches, insomnia and even dangerous disease like cancer. It is often one of the major reasons why women experience absence of menstruation.

People can often feel fatigue, various aches and pains, headaches and sleep disturbances because of excessive stress.

People who are under the effects of excessive stress will have more colds and infections due to lowered immune system responses.

Excessive Stress for a long period can lead to High Blood Pressure, Cancer, Heart disease, Diabetes, Asthma, etc.

Effect of Stress in Married Life:

Many people experience various sexual dysfunctions such as loss of desire as a result of Stress. People can become depressed or irritated which could also affect happy married life.

Most Common Reasons for Stress:

There could be hundreds of reasons for the Stress in people's life and Stressful situation may arise whenever we are not having adequate skill and knowledge to handle it.

However in my understanding two most common and fundamental reasons for stress in our life are:

(1) Our belief system about life that life is without any difficulties or obstacles, so whenever any difficult situation arises we get stressed.

(2) When our happiness depends too much on other people opinions.

We allow our happiness to depend on others views, opinions or on external factors. Have you ever heard this statement: "Don't do this or don't do that" because "What others will say or think?"

Consider the following example:

Zoe is a brilliant girl and works in a busy PR department in XYZ Company meeting various clients every day and loves to socialise. Whenever somebody compliments her about her look she feels good and happy, but whenever somebody says something negative about her she starts getting depressed and unhappy thinking something is wrong with her and she tries hard to get people appreciation.

In this way if she had 20 interactions in a day and 10 times people compliment her and 10 times they criticise her she would be feeling up and down throughout the day and would be getting disturbed at least 10 times a day which would lead to more stress because she is allowing others to control her happiness.

This situation leads us to a question: Who is controlling Zoe's life??? Well, the answer in this situation obviously is other people opinions are controlling Zoe's life. Now you need to ask yourself if other people are controlling your life as well and if yes then if this is the way you want to live your life?

Analysis:

In this situation, Zoe is living her life which is depending upon external factors and *her happiness depends upon other opinions and views* which most of the time would not be under her control i.e. Most of the time Zoe remains unhappy.

Another example:

I recently read this news and thought to share it with you: A Brazilian model is going for plastic surgery for the 42nd time!

The 36 years old model is preparing to have nylon wires implanted in her eyes to give them an oriental slant. She would be dancing ahead of a drum group of 300 people, hoping her sculpted beauty as a "percussion queen" will lead her samba team to the victory.

Well, it is nice to look good and hear when people give nice comments about your look however when the center of your happiness depends too much on other people opinion or comments, it will become the major cause of unhappiness after some time.

Analysis:

If you become obsessed with your looks and your happiness depends upon other people views then imagine what will happen after couple of years when people would stop appreciating your looks *as external beauty cannot remain same for years*. Then depression will follow.

"Mental tensions, frustrations, insecurity, aimlessness are among the most damaging stressors, and psychosomatic studies have shown how often they cause migraine headache, peptic ulcers, heart attacks, hypertension, mental disease, suicide, or just hopeless unhappiness."

--Hans Selye 1907-1982,

Symptoms and Stages of Stress

Following are some of the Stress Symptoms in Initial Stage:

a) Tension, Headaches

b) Insomnia

c) Fatigue

d) Feeling of Nervousness

e) High Blood Pressure

f) Irritation

etc.

So if you find any of the above symptoms in your life, you need to introspect that you may be under stress.

It is easy if you manage the stress in the initial stage, however if you allow stress to continue for a long time in your life it can produce disastrous effect on your health. It can lead to Depression, Sexual Problems, Migraine, Menstrual Distress, Panic Attack, etc.

At later stage Stress can results into: Cancer, Heart disease, Respiratory issues, Diabetes, Asthma, etc.

Ineffective way people try to cope with their Stressful situation.

Generally females if very stressed try to share their problems with friends to feel better and males try to keep it to themselves and try to figure out the situation from their own angle despite the fact whether they have the necessary skill to handle the situation or not.

Unfortunately the most common ineffective way people try to handle the Stressful situation is to avoid facing it. They believe if they do not face the situation for some time then maybe it would sort out on its own. They avoid talking about it, hate discussing it and fear to think about it which results the issue become more bigger.

To avoid facing the real problem or try to forget the real problem many people light a cigarette or drink to feel the sense of relief and calmness. Although it may bring a superficial sense of relief and calmness but the problem is not going to be solved by escaping from it.

Why people are not able to solve their Stress related problem?

Confusion:

Number one reason why people are not able to solve their stress problems is Confusion: Big Confusion is created at the time of problem and you just don't know what to do.

In my understanding *"when the problems come in life they do not come alone, often they come from all the possible areas of life at the same time "*and *"sometime problem gets too complex and confusion is created and you just don't know what to do"*.

Let's see following examples:

Consider a Stressful situation for an Entrepreneur Mr Phil:

Phil had a car accident and got hurt. The surveyor from Insurance company recommended repair workshop which would take about 3 months, creating transport issue for him as he has to travel a lot. Either he needs to purchase a new vehicle or take taxi for 3 months but both solutions would involve extra expenditure.

At the same time Phil also started losing the business for some reason, his investors started asking money back, he started having cash flow problem then got involved into physical fight which he didn't want to and then got involved with police station and court matters where he was not comfortable in handling the issue. The people to whom he knew and those to whom he has helped in their life stopped returning his phone calls.

His key employees are leaving the job. He is at risk of losing financially everything he had earned during his last 10 years working day and night and much more… and all this is happening at the same time and then the *confusion is created* and Phil just doesn't know what to do and how to get out of this situation.

Consider another Stressful situation in relationship for women:

Sarah is pretty, slim, tall and looks like a model. She fell in love with her batch mate Richard while studying at college. Sarah is doing part time job in a café while studying however she is ambitious and wants to study further to get a better job in the future.

After 2 years of dating, Sarah moved to Richard's flat and pays him rent as Richard told her that he is in some financial difficulty. She spends her savings on Richard's flat to make it look nicer.

She finds out that Richard does not want her to study further so she decided to stay with her job in a café as she does not want to lose Richard.

Both stayed together for 6 years. She loves Richard like anything and after 6 years Sarah feels that she is growing old and feels to settle down and she is waiting for the moment when Richard will propose to her. Sarah also took a personal loan for 7 years for refurbishing Richard's flat.

After waiting a long time Sarah expressed her desire to get married with Richard however he feels that he needs some more time. Time passes by, after another year Sarah again reminded Richard about marriage but somehow Richard expresses anger and said he needs to think as he does not want to make any commitment. Sarah does not want Richard to feel angry but at the same time she wants to settle down.

After some time Sarah becomes uncomfortable about Richard's activities as he regularly started going out late in the night and is busy answering late night calls which Sarah finds difficult to accept. She does not feel good and wants Richard to stop but he gets violent and sometimes even hits her whenever she tries to talk about his late night routine.

Richard stopped talking to her, she cries often and her health is going down, her work performance is seriously affected. Her boss has told her not to bring her house affairs into the office. She does not have the parental support & she felt totally broken.

One day Richard tells her that if she wants, she can leave him and he thinks that both of them are not made for each other. Sarah cries and cries and not sure what to do.

Sometimes he also brings her flowers and Sarah thinks that he may be stressed i.e. he hit her but actually he loves her and after some time he would change but somehow she start losing the connection.

She wanted to study but did not as Richard was not happy so she stuck with the small job in a cafe for years and now he doesn't want to live with her. She loves him and wants to get settle down but she does not want to stay unmarried.

She thought that Richard is deeply in love with her but when he started hitting her quite often, she is confused. She is still under the debts for the next couple of years which she has taken for refurnishing Richard's flat. She became *emotionally unsteady and totally confused* and does not know what to do.

Thinking a lot about problem

Another major reason that people are ineffective in solving their issues is, they worry too much about the events which are out of their control.

All the events which happen in our life can be divided into 2 categories:

(a)   The events on which we have control,

(b)   The events on which we have no control. (Example: *because of downsizing people get laid off, somebody very close to us gets injured in an accident or dies, get trapped in floods, etc*).

Most of the people who get Stressed and get into depression are the one who spend their time thinking on the events/issues which are out of their control and do nothing about those events which are under their control.

If you focus your mind on problem, the problem would become bigger and bigger and you get into circle of worrying and then your mind which is very interesting instrument starts playing its game.

Mind gives you the false impression that the problem is very big and not only that but it will also start multiplying your worries without any actual basis and gives you false impression that your problem is getting bigger and bigger and you see no way of coming out of it.

Your mind is even capable of creating new imaginary fear. There could be very high possibility that it would start creating various fears in your mind that some situation which you do not like is going to be true. The point to understand here is that most of the Stress is self created.

Self created Stress is caused because of the way we interpret the events or issues in our life. *A very common example can be that during the night somebody sees a snake and gets threatened without realizing that it may actually be a rope.*

Finally you enter into a state of depression with no hope of coming out of it. Then the only thing you think about most of the time is the problem and nothing else and you get more and more depressed.

"People who are not able to solve their Stress issues are those who devote too much time thinking about their *problems <u>only</u> rather than solution.*"

Failure to take decision

Finally people are not able to solve their Stress problem because they don't want to take decision and the reason for this is that somewhere in their mind there is some fear of failure and fear of something unknown which hold them back from coming out of stressful situation.

Because of confusion & fear of failure and not taking any decision, the problem gets more bigger and complex and in this process people get more stressed.

Part 2:

Understanding and Training our Mind

Life and Issues

Nowadays people get Stressed while dealing with all kind of situations even the simplest one.

The prime reason for this is somehow they are looking for perfection in everything and they believe that normal life is without any problem which is far from the truth.

Life is full of issues no matter what social status you enjoy in society, only the nature of issue would be different. You solve one issue, other would come and they would be keep on coming till you are alive. This is a reality and nobody can escape from this truth.

If you do not believe in this fact then think and please let me know who do you think does not have any problems/ issues in life?

Do you think people who are earning a lot like Investment Bankers are happy all the time? Maybe but what happens during recession or stock market crash? Market cannot be up all the time.

Do you think the Government Ministers and MP's are happy as they enjoy power and fame? Well, maybe but what happens when they lose the election after fixed term? One cannot be elected all his life and imagine what happens when you lose power and fame.

Who do you think does not have stress or issues in his/her life? Yeah, idea may come to your mind that maybe the spiritual gurus wearing orange cloths sitting in peaceful ashrams in India are happy and Stress free. What a wonderful discourse they deliver in front of people.

Don't be surprised to read what I am going to explain next that even in most of the so called spiritual organizations people live very stressful life and are angry inside.

Many people join these "spiritual organizations" because they find themselves very unhappy and they think that by joining them they can get peace. Well, they may experience some superficial peace but deep inside they have not dealt with their issues and the issues keep coming up and create anger and Stress.

They sing (chant) mornings and evenings thinking it would help them. Obviously when you are chanting your mind may get diverted from the actual problem and you may find some peace for the time being but problem/ issues are still there, i.e. peace on long term basis cannot be there unless you experience the ultimate truth within your own mind body realm.

Some people in India joined these "spiritual organizations" at young age when they were not ready for it. When they grow up their unfulfilled and suppressed desires are still there and will be increasing and the desires will keep disturbing them and it does not matter whether they wear orange cloths or not.

Most of those who joined at young age and stayed within the ashram environment developed depression as they haven't seen the outside world. The issue with them is they only recite stories which their gurus have taught them, have bookish knowledge and they only chant mornings and evenings.

Not only that but at the same time they are also tied up within the organization rules and regulations coupled with this is the organization politics. *Yes, I repeat organization politics even within "spiritual organizations".*

Question may come to your mind that why don't these people come out of spiritual centres? Well, during the years of growing up within the ashram environment *their confidence gradually broke down as they haven't faced the outside world.* Now think what happens to their peace of mind? The people who are living in most of so called "spiritual organizations" portraying themselves "confident" and "happy" to the outside world, talking about god, sacred stuff and nice stories are the one who are mostly Stressed.

What a terrible life, although these "orange clothed gurus" have perfected the art of telling nice mysterious stories and learned women psychology to manipulate them during these years but remain miserable and live life full of Stress.

This is the law of nature that every person who is born has to go through certain kind of painful experiences. The painful issues keep coming throughout life and would be affecting you till the point you start searching higher purpose of your life. As you progress on this path their impact become lesser and lesser and finally a stage would come where you can achieve liberation from Stress and unhappiness forever.

If you still think that your problem is very big, why not have a visit to any local hospital emergency ward and look around and see if your problem is still very big.

Still want to believe that your problem is very big? Then consider the following:

Let's say you think that you are earning or having less money than most of the people you know and you live a miserable financial life, then think about Incredible India, the world hottest economy where more than 70 percent people still live on less than one dollar a day and they are still managing to survive and it is not that they are all unhappy. I am sure you do not live on less than one dollar a day.

Let's say you often have cold or backache or joints pain, then think that you are still much better as approximately 20,000 people die of cancer every day worldwide.

By now you might feel angry thinking that you are feeling Stressed in your situation and I am giving you examples which have nothing to do with you or maybe thinking that I am trying to undermine your Stressful situation. Well, all I want to highlight is that *we all have one or another issue/problem in our day to day life.*

In my understanding *we all go through problems and frustrations at one stage or another, however the difference is how quickly we recover from them,* deal with them and learn lessons to make our life more fruitful and meaningful.

So understand and remember lesson No 1:

Life is full of Issues and they will keep coming till you are alive.

"One of the things I learned the hard way was it does not pay to get discouraged. Keeping busy and making optimism a way of life can restore your faith in yourself."

--Lucille Ball

Now the good news is:

No Problem / Issue is Permanent

Think about it what is permanent in this world.

Are you of same energy level as you were 10 years ago? Or

Does your face looks same as couple of years ago? Or Is your earning same as years ago? Or Do you have same problem in your life as you may had few years ago? Or

Does your city look same as years ago?

Nothing is same now as it was in the past. Nothing is permanent. Everything is changing, so would your problem.

Change is the law of nature. Nothing is permanent in this world. Accept it and you will be happy.

No matter what problem or issue you are having in your life at the moment, it would certainly change- but of course you need to take positive action too.

So understand and remember lesson No 2:

No Problem / Issue is Permanent

"People are always blaming their circumstances for what they are. I don't believe in circumstances. The people who get on in this world are the one who get up and look for the circumstances they want, and, if they can't find them, make them."

-- George Bernard Shaw

Developing a Habit of not Complaining

You need to develop a habit of not complaining. Normally people complain about everything in life. *People complain about cold weather during winter, about hot weather during summer and about rain in rainy season.* People who are single are depressed that they are single, those who are married think that singles are having more fun, people with darker skin want to get fair skin, people with white skin want tanning and the list never ends. Sometimes I think what would happen to people's life if you take their complaining habit out of their life?

What can you expect in rainy season? Of course... rain, what else! You can only experience coldness in winter so why complain. This is the law of nature.

Well, I am not saying that you should be complacent with wherever you are in your life and do nothing but you should enjoy what you have and keep moving ahead. By complaining you can only waste your time and condition your mind towards depression which will serve no purpose to you, rather pull you back in your life instead of moving ahead.

Do you want to know what will happen if you stop complaining? OK listen carefully now: if you stop complaining, you will progress in your life no matter where you are. It is always your choice either you spend your time and energy in discussing how

"I had no shoe and complained until I met a man who had no feet."

--Ancient Proverb

terrible life/ problem you are having or spent that time in coming out of your problem and fulfil your dreams.

So understand and remember lesson No 3

No Complaining from This Moment Onwards

Stay in Present Moment

Our uncontrolled mind plays a major part in making our life stressful.

If you observe the nature of human mind, it does not want to stay in present moment. It will either stay in the past or will run in the future and this is where the problem begins. If it goes into the past it may keep regretting about the past events in life and if it goes into future it become anxious about the future results.

Every thought drains energy. The more you dwell in anxious thought, the more your energy would be drained and your work related performance would be affected apart from affecting your health. Your craving for the future events also prevent you to enjoy what you have in the present.

So understand and remember lesson No 4

Train your mind to stay in the present moment *if you want to enjoy your life and live your life stress free.*

Desires

Mind has another interesting habit to produce countless desires. *Mind creates craving for whatever it does not have.* Each craving starts a mental agitation to achieve the result. Some people give this argument that by fulfilling desires, mind can be stress free. I agree yes it would happen but only for a short while. *If you observe the nature of mind you would come to realization that the moment one desire is fulfilled other desire would come up and so on and this process never stops.* When the desires exceed your capability to meet them, you start getting into stressful situation.

Now you may be thinking that I am going to give you a yogic advice - reduce all your desires and attachments and live Stress free life. Well, I would like to say that *"keep your desires under your capacity to meet them and you will live a happy life."*

So understand and remember lesson No 5

Keep your Desires under your Capacity to Meet them *and you will Live Stress Free Life.*

I cannot give you the formula for success, but I can give you the formula for failure--which is: "Try to please everybody."

--Herbert Bayard Swope

Be Internally Driven

We need to be internally driven. When somebody says something nice about me, it is good to hear those words. But at the same time if someone does not say those kind words or says something unpleasant, I need to remind myself that I am still a good human being and would not allow myself to feel down.

As Eleanor Roosevelt said *"No one can make you feel inferior without your consent"*. It's me who should decide about my happiness rather than others. When you feel down by other people comments, unknowingly you allow others to gain control over you.

I understand that what I just said is difficult, but it will remain mere theory if you do not practice it.

Remember that next time if anything unpleasant happens, just remind yourself that you don't have to feel bad and do not allow external circumstances to govern your happiness and make you Stressed. Rather you should be the one who is master of your life and decide about your happiness.

If centre of happiness stays within your control, you can stay happy and stress free to a great extent throughout your life.

Try to be internally driven. Let you should decide about your happiness or at least you should not totally depend on others appreciation otherwise sooner or later you will get into depression.

So understand and remember lesson No 6

Be Internally Driven

Train Your Mind for next 2 Weeks:

Week 1 Start Date: ....

Remember the Following	Sun	Mon	Tue	Wed	Thu	Fri	Sat
Life is full of issues							
No Complaining							
Stay in Present Moment							
Expense under Income							
Internally Driven							
No Problem is Permanent							

Train Your Mind for next 2 Weeks:

Week 2 from date: ....to ....

Remember the Following	Sun	Mon	Tue	Wed	Thu	Fri	Sat
Life is full of issues							
No Complaining							
Stay in Present Moment							
Expense under Income							
Internally Driven							
No Problem is Permanent							

Section 3:
5 Practical Steps for Managing Stress

First let me begin with the good news for you; if you are having any kind of difficult or depressive situation in your life then just try to chill out for a moment and smile please, yes smile please because I have a solution for it and I would help you to find it out for yourself.

Good, now as you smiling please remember my statement "If there is a problem then there has to be a solution". During my 38 years of life, I have come to this conclusion very strongly that for any depressive situation there has to be a solution though it is not necessary that solution will be obvious to you at that particular time. Now once you are ready let's start with step no 1.

Step No 1: "Identify the Causes of Stress"

There could be one problem or issue or there may be number of issues which may be causing Stress in your life. Your first step is to identify it. Sometime there could be number of minor issues which collectively can make life Stressful.

You need to identify them. I am giving you some guidelines below to think and see if the reason which is stressing you is from any of the following areas:

Work related Issues:

Stress situation can be because of fatigue and overwork: You may be working 7 days a week without giving yourself any rest. (Most often this is the situation with entrepreneurs or people working on shifts).

Impractical targets and planning: This can occur when you set up too high targets for yourself which you are trying to achieve in too little time. You need to check if your planning is ok.

Time Management Skills: Are your time management strategies effective? You need to record your time which you spend on various activities and see how much time you are wasting every day.

Job related skill: Are you lacking any job related skill or have inability to perform well in a particular role?

Job redundancy: Have you been redundant because your job has been outsourced?

Relationship Issues:

Do you have any fear that present relationship you are in would not work out in long term?

Do you have any fear that you are growing old and still you are single?

Do you think that you are having some extra weight and you don't feel confident with your partner or think that your partner may not like it?

Did you have bad relationship in the past and now when you are ready for new one you are having fear of falling into the same trap again?

Health Issue:

Are you losing your health and developing modern day lifestyle diseases like Insomnia, Diabetes, Heart related issues, etc?

Sudden Changes in Life:

Sudden changes in life- leaving home, job redundancy or getting married.

Social Situation:

Such as loneliness, or discrimination based on race, gender, age, or sexual orientation.

Surroundings:

If you live in a dangerous area where overcrowding, crime, pollution or noise is an issue.

Conflicts with your Belief System:

For instance, you lived your life under some belief system and just realised after years that the reality is something else. Now if you accept the reality then you have anger in your mind that you lived your life under wrong beliefs.

Hormonal Changes:

Women are particularly susceptible to Stress caused by hormonal changes. During puberty, pregnancy and menopause their hormone levels fluctuate consistently and cause stress.

Unreasonable Expectation:

If you have various unreasonable expectations which are unfulfilled, they can also create anger, disappointment and Stress in your life.

Desire more than your personal assets:

If your desires are more than your assets, you live a stressful life. For example you want to earn $ 3,00,000 a year but not able to earn more than $1,00,000. You would certainly live stressful life because you want a lifestyle of which your present income cannot match. Smartly Credit Card companies know this and take huge advantage of the situation, they allow you to buy much more than you can manage to pay effectively back and you get caught in the circle of paying high interest rate month after month and live in circle of debts.

There could be many more reasons for your stressful situation. What you need to do is to write down your thoughts and narrow them down.

I would suggest if you have many issues in your life, identify 3 main issues which are really disturbing your peace of mind.

Please do not go ahead, take a break now and write down the cause of your stress on the following page.

Step No 1: Identify the cause of your Stress NOW!

Step No 2: "Understand and Accept the Reality" that there is some real issue in your life which is disturbing your peace of mind and it really needs your attention.

Accepting the reality is very important and it is the next step in the direction of managing your stressful life. *Once you accept the reality then your mind can think further in the direction of solution.*

But if you do not accept it, you would be busy only in resisting the reality and getting Stressed. This would only make you more miserable and unhappy.

Let me explain with the help of an example why accepting the reality is a very crucial step in managing stress in your life. *Many people live year after year a very stressful life because they don't want to accept the reality.*

Case Study:

Mr John works in the government organization at a senior most position and manages hundreds of employees.

After a very successful career John retires from his job. Now after retirement John feels a big change in his life.

When John was in charge in his organization he got lots of attention, respect and well wishes regularly from big circle of friends who were always around him. Suddenly after retirement everything disappeared.

Mr John always believed that all the respect, honour and social status he enjoyed was all because of him and his hard work, however the reality is that everybody was around Mr John for their own selfish reason.

John health is falling down day by day. He has consulted number of doctors; they have done number of tests and prescribed him medicine. Although John is taking regular medication his blood pressure remains high most of the time, he is developing heart related problem, his hands shakes while writing, he was recently diagnosed for diabetes ....

Analysis:

John does not want to accept the reality that people were around him for their own selfish reason and not just because of him and he resists this.

This resistance creates lots of anger and Stress within him and he started losing his health despite the fact he is taking regular medicine. Most of his ill health is because of the Stress he is generating. His health can be improved once he accepts the situation and takes action. This way he would stop creating anger which is the main cause of his ill health.

Take a break now and accept the Stress Issues which you have identified.

Step No 2: Accept the Reality NOW- *Accept the Issue affecting your Life NOW.*

Step No 3: Collect all the Possible Information

Sometimes people are not able to solve their Stress problems because they do not collect enough information about the issue and they try to solve the issue with limited resources which they have and when they do not find proper solution they get Stressed.

Collect all the information about the main disturbing issues which you are not comfortable to handle. *In my experience it is very important to collect as much information as possible.* In fact many times you would be surprised to find out that many of the disturbing issues are simply solved while collecting the detailed information.

Introspect yourself if you have collected all the information which can help you in solving the problem and could define the problem accurately as much as possible.

Take a break Now and collect all the information as it is really important.

Step No 3: Collect Information NOW

Collect all the possible information regarding Stress issues which are affecting your life NOW and write them below.

"God loves to help him who strives to help himself."

--Aeschylus BC 525-456, Greek Dramatist

Step No 4: Focus your Attention on Solution

Write down and plan activities you need to perform to get out of Stress.

Focus your attention on solution.

I get the opportunity to interact with people from various cultural background, professions, from graduate Students to organizations Chairman.

One thing I observed very clearly is that *people who are mostly stressed in their life are the one who spend most of their time thinking about the problem.* They think more and more about problem and their mind magnify the problem of its own and they start worrying more and more.

I also noticed that people who are least stressed during problematic situations are the one who are solution and action oriented. They do think about the problem but most of the time they spend in solving the problem rather than only thinking about the problem.

Remember: *Nothing would happen unless you start concentrating on solution.*

In my understanding *the majority of people who get easily stressed are the one who think too much about their problem* **and the one who do not get stressed** *focus most of their time on solution* **and carry on.**

Example:

Susan thinks: I am already thirty eight and still unmarried so there may be something wrong with me. I may be overweight or I may not look good etc. These kind of thoughts are troubling her mind.

Now what do you think Susan is doing unknowingly?

Analysis:

She really wants to get married but rather than focussing her mind on solution, she is focussing on what she perceives as problem (not getting married) and she is unknowingly blocking the possibilities of marriage by thinking in a negative way. *It is the law of nature that wherever mind goes energy follows*. If you keep thinking that you cannot get married you are creating energy as not to get married.

Susan thinks: "I am overweight and that's why I am not getting married."

That's fine but what action she is taking to get rid of her extra weight. Is she working hard to become slimmer?

Lesson: Do not focus your mind too much on thinking about the problem rather *focus your mind on solution*.

If you really want to come out of stress, then start focussing your mind on solving the issue rather than only worrying about it.

Step No 4: Focus on solution NOW

Focus your mind on solution and write down all those activities which you can do of your own to come out of the problem or the possible solutions which are under your control and the *time frame* in which you planning to complete them.

Always Remember: **People fail to realise that things don't happen of their own, you have to make them happen.** *The issue will be solved only if you take decision and follow consistent action.*

Step No 5: Action

Managing Stress through Action: I would like you to focus your mind on the following statement: *"Nothing happens of its own, you have to make it happen"*.

So you need to be aware of the fact that if you really want to come out of Stressful situation or your depressing state of mind then you really need to take action.

Unless you stand up for yourself and take action, the stressful situation is not going to get away. Let the fear of failure should not stop you from taking action.

You might be thinking that it is easy to say when you are not into the problematic situation but very difficult to do and I would certainly agree with you but the point is there is no other way.

Some of you might have taken the action and then say: *"Yes I took the action and I am trying but nothing is happening."* Then think about the following saying:

"People keep on trying in the same way and they expect different result" Often happens that people try to solve their problem in the same way again and again and they expect different result which is not going to happen.

Have you tried other ways?

"Our greatest glory is not in never falling but in rising every time we fall."

-Confucius

Step No 5: Take Action NOW

Stress Management a Holistic Approach:

As we have read above that stress if continue to persist in our life for long time it can have disastrous effect on our health. Not only Stress de-energises you and makes you look older but also it can lead to fatal diseases like diabetes, ulcer, cancer, etc.

While you are working to tackle the main Stressful issue in your life which may take some time to sort out, it is very important that you release stress from your body and mind every day.

There has been enormous effort undertaken by present day medical science to handle the issue of stress. Stress is studied at the physical level by modern medical science, however modern medicine is not able to provide effective treatment to Stress because the real problem of stress does not lie in the physical body. It originates from the mind and then disturbs our energy level and finally appears on the physical level in the form of disease.

This is where many alternative activities like Yoga play an important part in releasing stress. *Follow the 5 steps as recommended in this book and some of the Stress releasing activities as described below and you will look young and energetic for long time to come.* **This is a holistic approach** *to handle any* **Stress issue** *in your life.*

Following are the few quick Stress releasing techniques which are quite effective. These methods would definitely help you to reduce Stress in short term and most importantly help you to avoid being caught in the ill effect of Stress.

Exercise

Regular physical activity is one of the effective ways to release Stress. You can do walking, mild exercise in a gym, swimming, etc.

Breathing Exercises

Deep breathing is an easy stress reliever that has numerous benefits for the body, including oxygenating the blood which 'wakes up' the brain, relaxing muscles and quieting the mind. Breathing exercises are especially helpful because they can be done anywhere and can quickly de-stress. Abdominal breathing and Yogic full breathing are good examples.

Meditation

When you are in a meditative state, it results in release of certain hormones that promote health.

Visualizations

One can imagine achieving goals like becoming healthier and more relaxed, doing well at tasks, and handling conflict in better ways. Visualizing can improve one's performance and help in relieving Stress at the same time.

Massage

This is another effective way to reduce stress. Try to get a massage from a friend or a professional. If neither is available, you can do a self message which will also work great in promoting circulation, releasing tension and helping you feel more relaxed.

Instant Relaxation Technique

By tensing and relaxing all the muscle groups in your body, you can relieve tension and feel much more relaxed in minutes, with no special training or equipment. Start by tensing all the muscles in your face, holding a tight grimace for 3 or 4 seconds, then completely relaxing for next few seconds. Repeat this with your neck, followed by your shoulders, your arms, your legs, etc. You can do this practice anywhere, and as you practice, you will find you can relax more quickly and easily.

Relaxing Music

The soft music can relax your body and calm your mind.

Writing

Research shows that expressing yourself in writing can be a very effective way to reduce Stress level.

Doing something you enjoy

A hobby or other healthy leisure activity that interest you can help you to relax (*Although when you are in terrible Stress situation you don't feel like doing anything but take my words for it and give it a try, it would definitely help you*).

Hatha Yoga

Hatha Yoga provides most effective approach to release Stress from body and mind. Major benefit of yoga is that it combines the practice of several Stress Management techniques such as Breathing, Meditation, and Visualization apart from Yoga Postures. One can begin with gentle yoga in the beginning and later on build up the strength for more advanced yoga postures.

"It is difficult to find happiness in oneself," "but it is impossible to find it anywhere else."

--Arthur Schopenhauer

Yogic Wisdom about Managing Stress:

Desire is the root cause of all unhappiness. You renounce your desires and attachment and you would be Stress free. When you reduce your worldly desires and attachment you can focus your mind inside and start knowing more about oneself.

Gradually you reach a stage where external events in your life can no longer disturb your peace of mind and there is only peace.

Our Published books:

Art of Breathing *for* Stress Free Life

The Only book on human breathing techniques for managing stress with clearly illustrated photographs and practical instructions. This book is ideal for busy people who lead a hectic life style.

Paperback /£4.95/ 56 pages

Gentle Yoga for 50 Plus

"A perfect gift of health for your parents"

The only book on Gentle Yoga for people in the age group of 50 plus. The exercises explained in this book are also beneficial if suffering from arthritis or rheumatism.

Paperback/ £5.95/68 pages

All our books are also available at Amazon.co.uk, Barnes and Nobles

Corporate Yoga

"The Only Book on Corporate Yoga"

This simplified book of corporate yoga has been written considering the need of people working in the corporate sector.

This book will help in relieving pain from lower back, neck, fingers and forearms. It will also help in making eye muscles stronger, releasing stress and keeping the blood pressure normal.

ISBN 978-0-9556882-2-5
Page 96 / Soft Cover / £19.95

Simplified Yoga for Golfers

The yoga plan in this book is carefully designed for people who play golf.

A strong and flexible body creates the foundation for injury-free golf game. Simplified Yoga poses described in this book will not only strengthen the muscles but will also help to bring flexibility.

Flexibility + Strength = Injury Free Golf Game

ISBN 978-0-9556882-3-2
Page 96 / Soft Cover / £24.95

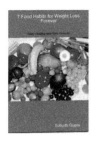

7 Food Habits for Weight Loss *Forever*

Stay Healthy and Slim *Forever*

"For anybody who wants to lose weight and gain health forever"

"Managing perfect body weight is not a complicated rocket science. Our body is made up of food which we eat during our day to day life. If we are overweight or obese at the moment then one thing is certain that the food which we eat is not good."

Healthy Food Habits = Good Health + Perfect Body weight *forever*

ISBN 978-0-9556882-0-1
Page 68 / Soft Cover / £4.95

Simplified Yoga for Backache

This book is a carefully designed practical guide for preventing and managing back pain.

Majority of back pain are caused by muscular insufficiency and lack of flexibility. A strong and flexible back creates the foundation for a healthy lifestyle.

Simplified yoga poses described in this book can be practiced by everybody, whether young or old, beginner or advanced. These poses will strengthen the back muscles and improve flexibility.

Page 68/ Soft cover/ £4.95

ISBN: 978-0-9556882-4-9

India Culture and Travel scams

"The only book on travel scams targeted at western tourists in India"

This is a practical book about understanding Indian culture and travel scams in India and is based on real life experiences.

This book will help you to avoid embarrassing mistakes and prepare you to feel confident in unfamiliar situations.

Content in this book includes Indian social customs, their perception about Western women, their religion, what motivates them, travel scams targeted at Western tourists and of course what not to discuss with Indians, etc.

Page 112/Paper Back / £5.95
ISBN 978-0-9556882-6-3

For more details please visit our website:
www.subodhgupta.com/books.html

All our books are also available at Amazon.co.uk, Amazon.com, Barnes and Nobles, Waterstones, WH Smith and Border.

Workshops and Yoga classes at workplace in London

We provide following workshops and yoga classes for Corporate Organizations and Celebrities in London.

(1) Regular Yoga Classes at work place for Managing Stresses.

(2) 4 hours workshop on Stress Management.

(3) Personal Stress Management Counselling.

For more details please contact:

Barbara Tomasik
Indian Foundation for Scientific Yoga and Stress Management
44(0)7966275913 (London)
info@subodhgupta.com, barbara@subodhgupta.com

www.subodhgupta.com